Food and
Noël Coward

Compiled by
Julie Vellacott

Food and Noël Coward
Julie Vellacott

First published in Australia by Julie Vellacott 2023
www.julievellacott.au

A catalogue record for this
book is available from the
National Library of Australia

ISBN: 978-0-6457494-0-3 (pbk)
ISBN: 978-0-6457494-1-0 (ebk)

Typesetting and design by Publicious Book Publishing
Published in collaboration with Publicious Book Publishing
www.publicious.com.au

To my friends who encouraged me to write this book.

LIST OF CONTENTS

INTRODUCTION

Food and Noël Coward is a tribute to a man who has long been part of my life. From an early age I was dazzled by stories of his style and wit. My much-loved oldest brother Lance and friends sang his songs around the piano. *Private Lives* was one of the first live performances I attended; from then on, I was addicted to the theatre and deeply interested in the enigmatic Sir Noël Coward.

Everything I read showed me a man bursting with talent and enthusiasm, who was confident and disciplined, who worked hard and enjoyed life.

This is no scholarly analysis of the man and his work; it's a light-hearted look at some of the food he wrote about. I started to invent a list of things I would cook if Sir Noël came to dinner, and it went on from there. I have read most of Noël Coward's written work and have a collection of first editions and memorabilia. His interest in food was evident from the first reading. Most writers include food in their writing, but his use of food and drink is so detailed and exactly right I believe it had a special meaning for him. This is one of the things I hope comes through in this book.

Food has been an obsession privately and in my working life. I have been lucky enough to work with some of the best in the field and never tire of learning; of increasing my understanding of the part good food plays in a full and rich life.

As well as writing plays and performing in them, Noël Coward wrote songs, music, short stories, poetry and novels. He wrote, directed and acted in several films. He was an artist and a cabaret performer.

I hope that his many admirers, people who enjoy food and cooking, theatre and entertainment, wit, humour, travel - most people in fact - will enjoy this book. There are those, like me, who seek out food references in every book they read; every play or film they watch. I'm disappointed whenever a meal is mentioned but no details provided.

The celebrations for the centenary of Noël Coward's birth on December 16, 1999, contributed to a huge upsurge in his popularity. In a British poll held in 1999, only Shakespeare was ahead of Noël Coward in the playwright popularity stakes. *Brief Encounter* was voted second most popular British movie. His most famous play, *Private Lives*, is continually performed throughout the world. 2023 marks fifty years since his death on 26 March 1973 at Firefly, his home in Jamaica.

In 1999 I was living in Singapore and had time on my hands while waiting for a working visa. I knew Noël Coward had visited Singapore several times and Raffles Hotel had a suite named after him. On visiting, imagine my dismay when on the wall was a photograph of a bearded gent with the caption *Noël Coward*. (Who was that man? I never did find out.) The hotel didn't have any other photographs of him, so I did some research.

I found the Centenary web page curated by the Noël Coward Society – now replaced by the official Noël Coward page. https://www.Noëlcoward.com/

Action was taken and on my next visit to Raffles there was the Master, gazing out serenely. I joined the Society and tentatively suggested to other members that it might be fun to do a Noël Coward cookbook. Some were keen, although rather sceptical about the type of food it might involve. I managed to convince them and myself that the food references I remembered from Noël Coward's written work, diaries and biographies were worth documenting.

Noël Coward's long-time friend Graham Payn described his eating habits, 'He was literally a meat and potatoes man, so meals were nothing elaborate. Bangers-and-mash was a perennial favourite for lunch, and in the evening a light snack before an early night and a book in bed.'

This was discouraging. I couldn't base a cookbook on meat and potatoes, bangers-and-mash and light snacks. I decided to read all the written material by and about Noël Coward that I could find. As well as whiling away the time pleasantly this reinforced my conviction that there was a lot more to the Master's eating and cooking habits than British stodge. He had a nice feel for food, he enjoyed eating and he deplored badly prepared or inappropriate food. In his later years he became a slightly eccentric but competent cook.

It's not surprising that Noël Coward took up cooking and enjoyed it. Cooking is creative and reminiscent of performing on stage – the response is instantaneous; there are no second chances.

It's worth noting that he lived through two world wars - with the associated food shortages - and in the early 1900s it simply wasn't the done thing to be overly interested in food. Cooks were there to do the cooking, and servants to serve it. It was considered rather vulgar to notice or comment on what you were eating. In the Coward household the young Noël *did* notice food. When his mother decided to supplement the family income by taking in paying guests, they had to be catered for. He writes that 'Emma (our beloved "General") was still with us and she was a good cook.'

Following World War II attitudes and habits changed. Famous people not previously associated with cooking and food wrote cookbooks. Noël Coward wrote a foreword to *Delightful Food* by Marjorie Salter and Adrianne Allen Whitney, published in1957. He also provided a recipe for 'Our Favourite Dish – the theatre recipe book' compiled by Mrs Prince Littler in aid of the Actors' Orphanage.

One of the joys of researching this book has been delving into cookbooks from the early part of the twentieth century. Most of the recipes were written for experienced cooks who had no fear of using their own judgement when it came to quantity, oven temperature or tin size. I have amended this aspect. The recipes in this book are typical of the era in which they are described in the writings.

'Up until this year I had always appreciated good cooking but never tried to cook and the only pronouncement I had hitherto made on the subject was "If it's rissoles I shan't dress", a rule I made in 1929 and to which I still strictly adhere.' (*From the foreword to Delightful Food*)

This book combines two things that have given me a lot of pleasure over the years – cooking and Coward. I have let the quotes create a sense of the occasion on which the food in this book was mentioned, and hopefully given a glimpse into the complex and captivating personality of Noël Coward.

'The most important ingredients of a play are life, death, food, sex and money – but not necessarily in that order.'

A LITTLE SOMETHING ON A TRAY

Joyce: Colds are fun.

Bobbie: She loves having a fuss made of her, beef tea – chicken – jelly with whipped cream – and fires in her bedroom, little Sybarite.

(The 'odd messes of bright pink jelly with whipped cream on top … arranged daintily in glass dishes.' which Noël ate in the army canteen reappear in *I'll Leave it to You*.)

Noël is, of course, describing himself here. He loved the luxury of retiring to bed with a 'little something on a tray'. The fact that this scene was far removed from his public high-living image probably added an extra fillip to his enjoyment of it. He had the happy ability to take pleasure in the little things, the 'small delights'.

John…Can you remember our small delights? How exciting they were? Sleep, warmth, food, drink, unexpected comforts snatched out of turmoil, so simple in enjoyment, and so incredibly satisfying.

Post-Mortem

Beef Tea

1 lb / 500g beef – shin or chuck
1 pint / 600ml water
Pinch of salt

1. Trim fat from meat and cut into small pieces.

2. Place beef, water and salt into the top of a double boiler, bring to the boil then simmer very gently for 2 hours.

3. Strain and skim off any fat. Serve hot.

Creamed Chicken

3 lb / 1½kg whole chicken
1 small onion, peeled
bouquet garni
1 onion, finely chopped
8 fl oz / 250ml cream
1 egg yolk
2 oz / 60g butter
salt and pepper
chopped parsley

1. Put chicken, whole small onion and bouquet garni into a saucepan. Cover with boiling water and simmer for about 1½ hours until tender.

2. When chicken is cool enough to handle, take all meat off the bones and dice. Strain cooking liquid and skim off any fat. Reserve for soup or sauces.

3. Heat the butter in a deep fry pan and sauté the chopped onion until soft. Add the chicken and enough of the cooking liquid to moisten, about half a cup.

4. Beat together the egg yolk and cream, stir into chicken mixture and heat gently, being careful not to let it boil. Season to taste with salt and pepper.

5. Spoon over hot toast or rice and sprinkle with chopped parsley.

Sunday 16th December 1951, at Goldenhurst. 'Probably the nicest birthday I have ever had.... Bed at ten o'clock with kidneys and bacon on a tray. Utterly exhausted but deeply and profoundly happy. I am home again.'

The Noël Coward Diaries

Kidneys and Bacon

2 lamb's kidneys
4 rashers bacon
1 shallot, finely diced
¼ cup stock or water or wine
Butter
Chopped parsley
Salt and pepper
Worcestershire sauce

1. Heat a heavy fry pan and cook bacon to preferred crispness. Remove from pan and keep warm.

2. Core and skin kidneys, cut in half.

3. If there is not enough bacon fat to sauté kidneys, add a little butter. Sauté kidneys in pan until lightly browned all over. They should still be slightly pink inside. Remove and keep warm.

4. Add shallots to the pan and cook for about a minute, stirring occasionally, until soft.

5. Add stock, water or wine and bring to the boil, scrape up pan juices. Boil for 2 minutes or until reduced by half. Check seasoning, add salt and pepper and a dash of Worcestershire sauce.

6. Return kidneys and bacon to the pan and heat gently for a few minutes.

7. Serve on hot toast, pour over pan juices and garnish with chopped parsley. To vary serve with a few mushrooms, sliced and sautéed in the bacon fat, or a well-grilled tomato.

8. Makes 1 generous serve.

'He loved supper in bed at the end of these White Cliffs days, the noise of the sea so close to his bed; "a little something eggy on a tray," …'

Remembered Laughter

These are my favourite little eggy somethings, and I like to think Noël would have enjoyed them too.

Eggs en Cocotte

Butter a fireproof ramekin, break 2 eggs into it, pour in a little cream, and sprinkle with salt and pepper.
Bake in a moderate oven for 6-8 minutes.
Some grated cheese can be sprinkled over the top, or some chopped ham placed at the bottom.

Creamy Scrambled Eggs
To each egg allow ½ oz butter and 1 tablespoon cream. Melt the butter in a saucepan, add the eggs beaten with the cream and some salt, pepper and a dash of Tabasco.

Stir constantly over low heat until almost set, but still slightly runny, as the eggs will continue cooking after being removed from pan.

Serve accompanied by hot buttered toast.

Chopped parsley can be added to the eggs during cooking.

Luxury Eggs

Scrambled eggs, cooked as above.

Put a few strips of smoked salmon on a toasted and buttered English muffin. Spoon scrambled eggs over and top with a generous teaspoonful of caviar.

Good for breakfast, lunch or supper.

Eggs with Potato Puree

Poached eggs on a very hot, very buttery and peppery puree of potatoes. Elizabeth David calls this "delicious invalid food", but you don't have to be an invalid to enjoy it. Good for when you feel a little jaded and need some comforting.

Omelette (for one)

2 eggs
1 dessertspoon cold water
½ oz / 15g butter
salt and pepper

1. Beat the eggs and water with a fork or whisk until frothy. Add the salt and pepper.

2. Heat the butter in a small (about 20cm/8") omelette pan until very hot but not brown. Pour in egg mixture and turn down the heat to medium.

3. Tilt the pan while lifting the edge of the omelette with a spatula, so the uncooked egg mixture runs underneath. Do this several times.

4. When set but still moist, which takes only a couple of minutes, fold in half and cover the pan for 30 seconds.

5. Slide onto a warm plate to serve.

Variations: Add chopped ham, chives, parsley or grated cheese to mixture before pouring into pan.

Spoon sautéed mushrooms or tomatoes onto omelette just before folding.

I can't resist adding 'Warsaw Concerto', a recipe Noël Coward contributed to *Our Favourite Dish – the theatre recipe book.* No quantities are provided – the recipe is exactly as shown in the book.

Eggs
Onions
Vinegar
Breadcrumbs
Butter
Seasoning

Cut the onions into thin slices and fry in butter until brown. Add a little vinegar and continue frying from three to five minutes. Grease a fire-proof dish and line with onions.

Slide in the required number of eggs, unbroken, add salt and pepper and cover generously with bread-crumbs.

Dab top with bits of butter and grated cheese. Bake in hot oven for five to six minutes, when eggs should have set.

'…We learned that Cadbury's Bournvita ensured sound and restful sleep and we faithfully drank it or Horlick's or Ovaltine, last thing every night, Noël sitting up in bed and wondering what his fans all over the world, who pictured him constantly sipping champagne, would think of the reality.

Then we switched to slightly more sophisticated sleep-inducers, such as jasmine or mint tea, or tisanes of *tilleul* or *fleurs d'oranger…*'

'Let's have a Tisane for Twosane at half-past ten.'

Remembered Laughter

'They all went to a jolly night-club and I went, gratefully, to my jolly bed.'

The Noël Coward Diaries

BREAKFAST

'…he ate the breakfast Kitty had prepared; a cooked one, most often his favourite grilled pork sausages with bacon, extravagantly splashed with Worcester Sauce.'

Noel Coward and His Friends

Sausages and bacon were favourites at any time of day. The first mention of Noël actually cooking occurs when he was a young man on his own in New York. 'I was penniless and very lonely…. I used to get packets of bacon, on credit, from the Italian grocer just near the studio, and cook it sparingly in the kitchenette.'

Present Indicative

Turner: Would you like bacon and eggs after your grape-fruit, ma'am? Or eggs without bacon, or bacon without eggs?
Janet: I suppose there aren't any sausages, are there?

Home Chat

Any Part of Piggy
(from Not Yet the Dodo)

Any part of piggy
Is quite all right with me
Ham from Westphalia, ham from Parma
Ham as lean as the Dalai Lama
Ham from Virginia, Ham from York,
Trotters, sausages, hot roast pork.
Crackling crisp for my teeth to grind on
Bacon with or without the rind on
Though humanitarian
I'm not a vegetarian.
I'm neither crank nor prude nor prig
And though it may sound infra dig
Any part of darling pig
Is perfectly fine with me.

Sandra: 'I really must apologise for this barbarous idea of George's of having communal breakfast. He saw a country-house comedy once in which everyone was frightfully witty all through the last act and kept on helping themselves to kedgeree. My God, there really *is* kedgeree.'

South Sea Bubble

Kedgeree

½ onion, chopped
1 teaspoon turmeric
2 oz / 60g butter
2 cups cooked long grain rice
1 cup cooked, flaked smoked haddock (or other fish)
2 hard-boiled eggs, chopped
1 tablespoon chopped parsley
salt and pepper
pinch of cayenne pepper
extra butter

1. Sauté the onion and turmeric in half the butter until transparent.

2. Stir in the rice and the rest of the butter.

3. Add the fish, eggs, salt, pepper and cayenne. Fold in carefully so all the ingredients are evenly mixed.

4. Cover and reheat very gently.

5. Dot with pieces of extra butter and sprinkle with chopped parsley.

Serves 4 – 6.

More about the bacon obtained on credit. In New York, during a hot summer in 1921, '...I found it more comfortable, when actually frying, to be stark naked. This aroused the moral indignation of a cop, who had been observing me from the other side of the street, and he came and banged loudly on the door. I put on a dressing gown and ran downstairs with the bacon fork still in my hand and upon opening the door received the full force of his rage, which evaporated quickly when I asked him if he would care for a little red wine. He came up into the studio and polished off three glasses…'

Present Indicative

At Spithead Lodge in Bermuda Noël cooked his own breakfasts…' of which he was very proud. He performed some terrible experiments in the kitchenette, sprinkling his breakfast coffee with grated chocolate and then adding a large pinch of cinnamon the idea of which, first thing in the morning, made us fee faintly sick, but which he strongly recommended.'

Remembered Laughter

LUNCH & SUPPER

Alec: Shall we lunch nosily or quietly?
Janet: Oh, quietly.

Home Chat

During 1912 the young actor 'spent a lot of time going the round of the agencies.'
Never one to refuse hospitality, even when unintentional, he had already developed definite standards regarding food and opportunism.

'I had sixpence to spend on lunch which I took, not in an ordinary Lyons, but in the Corner House. Macaroni and tomato sauce fourpence, a roll a penny, and a penny for the waitress. Sometimes I was fortunate enough to find fourpence under the plate when I arrived at the table. This meant a chocolate éclair extra and twopence for the waitress.'

As a struggling young playwright, he was grateful for the hospitality of friends. 'I went to a lot of lunch parties in the most charming houses…I have a uniform memory of …eggs, mushrooms, cutlets, sausages, and bacon sizzling in casserole dishes. The conversation, I am sure, was distinguished… I only remember that I felt happy and confident and very pleased to be eating such nice food with such nice people.'

Present Indicative

In later years he became more critical.

'On Friday Edith Evans and I were hosts at a luncheon (so-called) to the Comédie Française …the lunch was quite, quite inedible. The sheer British bloody impertinence in offering a group of French visitors that disgusting meal is beyond belief. I felt bitterly ashamed. The French behaved charmingly and, in spite of the diced beetroot, tastelessly dusty mousse, soggy lettuce and stale cream buns, seemed to enjoy themselves.'

The Noël Coward Diaries

Noël, at the tender age of fifteen, toured as Charley in *Charley's Aunt*. It was not a well paid role, as he notes in *Present Indicative*" Often I had only enough money for one meal a day…after the show at night…I stuffed myself with fish and chips."

Of course, it's easier to find a good chippy. But worth making at home.

Fish and Chips

1½ lb / 675g cod fillets (or other firm white fish)
2 tablespoons lemon juice
Salt and cayenne pepper
6 medium-sized potatoes
2 tablespoons plain flour
Oil for deep frying
2 lemons cut into wedges
Beer batter (see recipe following)

1. Cut fish into serving pieces, 2 or 3 pieces per serving.

2. Place fish on a plate and sprinkle with lemon juice, salt and pepper. Leave to marinate while you prepare the chips.

3. Wash and peel the potatoes, cutting them into strips about 3"/ 7.5cm long. Rinse in cold water and drain thoroughly. Pat dry with clean tea towel.

4. Heat oil to 375°F/190°C. Fill frying basket one-half to two-thirds full of potatoes and immerse it gently into the hot oil. Shake the basket occasionally to keep the potatoes from sticking together. Fry until potatoes are almost cooked. Drain off excess oil and spread on a tray lined with paper towels to absorb excess oil while you fry the rest of the chips.

5. Sift flour, salt, ground pepper and a pinch of cayenne pepper on to a flat dish. Dust the fish with the flour mixture.

6. Dip the fish pieces into the batter one at a time as required.

7. Deep fry fish in oil at 375°F/190°C until crisp and golden. Place fish in a pan lined with paper towels and keep warm.

8. Heat the oil to 375°F/190°C again and refry potato chips in small batches until golden brown. Drain.

9. Serve fish and chips together in a heated serving platter. Garnish with lemon wedges.

Serves 4 – 6

Beer Batter

6 oz / 175g plain flour
½ teaspoon salt

2 tablespoons olive oil
¼ pint / 150ml beer
2-4 tablespoons water
1 egg white

1. Sift the flour and salt into a bowl, make a well in the centre.

2. Pour in olive oil and gradually add beer, stirring with a wooden spoon to mix in flour from sides of well. Batter should be completely smooth and of the consistency of thick cream. Add water to thin if needed. Leave to rest for 1-2 hours.

3. When ready to use batter whisk the egg white until stiff and fold in gently but thoroughly.

'Though rather frail and wobbly' (following a bout of pneumonia) Noël took 'the family' to the Boxing-Day matinee of *Peter Pan*. '… Next day, undaunted, we took Kay Kendall to the Caprice, where we ate two enormous helpings of steak-and-kidney pudding, and then, distended, to see *Where the Rainbow Ends*, which reeked with nostalgia for us all…'

The Noël Coward Diaries

Steak and Kidney Pudding

1½ lb / 750g rump steak
1 ox kidney
1 onion, diced
4 fl oz / 125ml beef stock or water
1 tablespoon Worcestershire sauce
Some flour, seasoned with salt and freshly ground pepper

1. Butter a 2½ pint / 1½ litre pudding basin.

2. Cut the steak into 2cm cubes. Clean the kidney and cut into small pieces. Toss the steak and kidney pieces in seasoned flour.

3. Roll our suet crust (see recipe following) and line the pudding basin, leaving enough to cover the top.

4. Add the meat, onion, Worcestershire sauce and stock or water. Add a few oysters for a special touch

5. Place the suet crust on top of the pudding, moistening the edges and pressing them firmly together.

6. Put a piece of buttered baking paper over the top, then cover with a piece of pleated foil or greaseproof paper. Tie down well. Note: Don't use a tightly fitting lid, as the pudding will expand slightly over the top of the basin.

7. Place in large pot, add boiling water halfway up pudding basin. Steam for 3 hours, checking frequently that pudding does not boil dry.

8. Traditionally steak and kidney pudding is served in the basin with a white napkin tied around OR leave to cool for a few minutes then turn out onto a hot serving dish.

9. A little port can be added just before serving – make a small hole in the top of the pudding and pour in.

10. Serve with mashed potatoes and green vegetables.

Serves 6.

Suet Crust
(Enough for one steak and kidney pudding)

8 oz / 250g plain flour
4 oz / 125g shredded suet
1 teaspoon baking powder

¼ teaspoon salt
About ½ cup cold water

1. Sift the flour, baking powder and salt into a bowl.

2. Add the suet and mix well.

3. Using your hands to squeeze the dough together, mix in some enough cold water to make a stiff dough which leaves the sides of the bowl clean.

'This was even greater fun to do at night: to dine off cheese fondue in the hotel and then come racing down under a full moon, a sky full of stars, and lights twinkling from the chalets on the white mountainsides. Noël loved it, having been what he called "a speed merchant" all his life…'

Noël Coward and His Friends

Cheese Fondue

1. Allow about 6 oz / 200g of Gruyere or Emmenthal cheese and a wineglassful of dry white wine per person.

2. Rub the inside of your fondue pot or saucepan with a clove of garlic, and put in a knob of butter.

3. Melt butter over low heat, and add the cheese which has been grated, plus half the wine.

4. Let the cheese melt and come to a gentle simmer, stirring occasionally. When it is smooth and very hot, add the rest of the wine. It should have the consistency of pancake batter.

5. Have ready for each person a few slices of good crusty French bread. Everyone should have a long-handled fork at the ready for dipping the bread in the cheese.

6. The fondue pot should be placed in the centre of the table and kept hot with a spirit lamp or candle.

7. Dip the pieces of bread in the cheese, twirl around to tidy up the strands of cheese and eat it off the fork.

At Goldenhurst, Lord Boothby (a neighbour) '…was going through a period of trying to popularise the herring. These he gave weekly to Noël in wooden boxes and, rolled in oatmeal, gently grilled and served with mustard sauce, they were delicious; all friends were made – were in fact delighted – to eat them.'

Remembered Laughter

Grilled Herrings with Mustard Sauce

Clean required number of herrings, dip in seasoned beaten egg and roll in fine oatmeal.
Arrange in buttered baking dish and place under a moderately hot grill for 10-15 minutes. Grill until golden brown. Turn once only during cooking.

Mustard Sauce

1 oz / 30g butter
1 oz / 30g plain flour
1 teaspoon mustard powder
salt and pepper
8 fl oz / 250ml milk

1. Melt butter in saucepan, stir in flour and mustard powder and cook gently for 1 minute until smooth.

2. Add the milk and bring to the boil, stirring or whisking continuously. Simmer for 5 minutes.

About 4 serves.

Variation: Omit mustard powder, add a teaspoonful of prepared English or Dijon mustard to the plain white sauce.

When Noël was in America in 1921 he met and made friends with the Lunts, whom he often visited at their 'shabby, congenial rooms'.

'We discussed, the three of us, over delicatessen potato salad and dill pickles, our most secret dreams of success. …Lynn and Alfred … were to become idols of the public … they were to act exclusively together. … when all three of us had become stars of sufficient magnitude…we would meet and act triumphantly together.'

Noël Coward and His Friends

Their dream came true twelve years later with *Design for Living*.

Potato Salad and Dill Pickles

2 cups cooked cubed potatoes, warm
1 teaspoon grated onion
½ stalk celery, finely sliced
½ teaspoon salt
½ cup French dressing (mix 2 parts olive oil to 1 part white wine vinegar, add a pinch of salt and pepper)
1 hard-boiled egg, chopped
½ cup sliced dill pickles
1 cup of mayonnaise

1. Mix together the potatoes, onion, celery, salt and French dressing. Leave to stand for at least an hour.

2. Gently fold in the egg, pickles and enough mayonnaise to bind all the ingredients together.

3. Serve in lettuce cups, with extra dill pickles on the side. Very good on its own or with cold meats.

Serves 4.

'We sat in the garden under oleander trees and had barbecued hotdogs and potato pancakes with chives and sour cream, and it was delicious and peaceful and I stayed cheerfully until dawn.'

Potato Pancakes

4 medium potatoes, raw
1 tablespoon plain flour
2 eggs, well beaten
½ teaspoon salt
freshly ground pepper
1 small onion, grated
Oil or bacon fat for frying
approx. 1 cup sour cream
bunch of chives

1. Grate potatoes into a bowlful of cold water. Drain and press out as much water as possible.

2. Mix together with flour, eggs, salt, pepper, and onion.

3. Heat 2 tablespoons of oil or fat in heavy frypan until very hot.

4. Drop tablespoons of mixture into pan, press down lightly and cook for a couple of minutes on each side.

5. Remove from pan and keep warm.

6. Spoon sour cream onto each pancake and sprinkle with snipped chives.

Delicious with ham, bacon or barbecued hotdogs. Can also be served with apple or cranberry sauce.

'Noël's dressing room was usually full to bursting, and afterwards most of us would repair to what was known by every actor in Paris as the Club, just off the Rond Point, for onion soup or *oeufs au beurre noir* and a few drinks.'

Remembered Laughter

French Onion Soup

4 large onions, sliced
2 oz / 60g butter
1 tablespoon plain flour
4 cups beef stock or water
salt and freshly ground black pepper
4 thick slices of French bread, toasted
grated parmesan cheese

1. Melt the butter in a large pan and cook the onions until soft.

2. Stir in the flour and cook for 1 minute.

3. Add stock or water and heat to boiling, stirring occasionally. Simmer for 30 minutes.

4. Season to taste with salt and pepper.

5. Place a slice of toasted bread in each individual ovenproof bowl. Pour over the soup and sprinkle with cheese.

6. Put into hot oven for a few minutes to melt and brown the cheese.

Serves 4

Eggs with Beurre Noir

2 eggs
3 tablespoons butter
1 tablespoon wine vinegar

1. Heat 1 tablespoon butter in frypan until very hot. Break eggs into a saucer and slide into pan.

2. When egg white begins to set, shake the pan to prevent eggs from sticking.

3. Pour a few drops of boiling water into the pan and cover. Turn off heat and leave until eggs are cooked to desired firmness.

4. Remove eggs to serving plate and keep warm.

5. Brown the remaining butter in the same pan, stir in the vinegar and pour over the eggs.

Serves 1

Ian Fleming, Noël's neighbour at Blue Harbour, reported that "…Coley has to spend half the day running up and down (to Firefly) …with…hot dishes of quiche Lorraine!"

Noël Coward: A Biography

Noël wrote a foreword to Marjorie Salter & Adrianne Allen Whitney's book 'Delightful Food' – published in 1956. Possibly the quiche he enjoyed was made using this recipe from that publication.

Quiche Lorraine
(from *Delightful Food*)

Line a tart plate with a good short paste. Make some cuts in the dough with a knife, then cover the bottom with thin slices of grilled bacon and then large thin slices of Gruyere cheese. Fill with a custard made as follows: 2 eggs with salt and pepper, well beaten with a fork. To this is added 1 cup of milk or cream. Place the pie in a very hot oven so that it starts to bake, then lower the heat to complete the baking for about 25 minutes.

Here is a basic recipe for

Plain Short Pastry
8 oz / 250g plain flour
Pinch of salt
4 oz / 125g butter (or pastry shortening)
about ¼ cup iced water

1. Sift flour and salt into a mixing bowl. Add butter, cut into cubes with flat-bladed knife.

2. Mix quickly, rubbing with your fingertips until mixture resembles breadcrumbs.

3. Sprinkle over iced water, stirring in with a flat-bladed knife until the pastry pulls together into a ball and leaves the bowl clean. Add extra water if required. Wrap dough in cling film and chill for 15 minutes.

4. Roll out to required size.

5. Enough for two 9"/23cm pie shells.

'The supper routine during the run of *The Vortex* is one of my pleasantest memories.

…The Gargoyle was practically next door to the Royalty Theatre and specialised in sausages and bacon and a small dance band consisting of a pianist and a trap-drummer who caressed, tenderly, the latest tunes, without imposing the slightest strain either upon the ears or the digestive tract.'

Present Indicative

Cole Lesley states 'I was by now an efficient all-round cook except that I scrupulously avoided anything to do with flour; the making of pastry, pies, cakes and soufflés to this day remains to me a deep mystery, and all these were the things Noël particularly liked to eat.'

Remembered Laughter

Earlier that year Noël had written in his diary, 'This afternoon I am going to the Lunts to be taught how to make pies!'

Some time later he wrote 'I have cooked most of the meals and am really becoming quite good. I have, I think, mastered the simpler forms of pastry-making and have made several exquisite pies, both savoury and sweet. It is enormous fun and I am enjoying myself.'

The Noël Coward Diaries

Typically, Noël put a tremendous amount of effort into mastering a new skill. In the foreword to *Delightful Food,* he recalls '…the thirty-six hours I spent first trying to make puff pastry, during which I had to cancel all engagements and lost a night's sleep into the bargain…'

Puff Pastry

8 oz / 250g plain flour
8 oz / 250g cold butter
Cold water
Pinch of salt

1. Sift flour and salt into a bowl and mix in just enough cold water to make a spongy dough.

2. Roll out into an oblong shape on a floured board. Leave to rest for 15 minutes.

3. Flatten the butter to about a 1"/2½cm thickness. Put in one piece in the middle of the pastry and fold the pastry sides and ends over it. Pinch or roll the edges together to seal in as much air as possible.

4. Leave for 15 minutes, then roll into a long strip. Fold in four, roll again and leave to rest for 15 minutes.

5. Turn pastry, repeat folding and rolling 6 or 8 times, making sure the edges are well-sealed each time. Leave to rest for 15 minutes in a cool place between each turn.

Sufficient for one pie top or 24 vol-au-vent cases.

Vol-au-vent cases

1. Roll out puff pastry to about ¾"/2cm thick.

2. Cut into rounds with a crinkly cutter about 2"/5cm in diameter.

3. Using a 1"/2½cm cutter cut another circle in the centre of each round, being careful to only cut through half the thickness of pastry.

4. Press down the centre circles and prick with a fork to prevent rising.

5. Place on baking sheets in a preheated oven and bake for about 25 minutes at 400°F/200°C. Pastry should be firm and slightly golden.

6. Cool on wire cake rack. Remove any excess pastry in centre before filling.

7. If you want lids for your vol-au-vents, cut them out of extra pastry rolled thinly, brush with beaten egg and bake as above.

Cole Lesley in *Remembered Laughter* recalls an occasion when Noël was cooking dressed only in a plastic apron patterned with rosebuds. The Bishop of Bermuda paid a surprise visit and was treated to the sight of Noël bending over to check the progress of his vol-au-vents.

Some vol-au-vent fillings:

Flake some cooked fish or crab, season with lemon juice, salt, pepper and a pinch of cayenne. Stir in a beaten egg yolk and enough cream to bind the mixture together. Spoon into prepared cases and bake in hot oven for 3-4 minutes.

Thin down some white sauce with a little cream. Add one or a mixture of the following: shredded cooked chicken or ham, sliced cooked asparagus or mushrooms, cooked prawns or shrimps. Season with lemon juice, grated lemon zest, salt, pepper, cayenne, chopped chives or parsley. Spoon into cases and bake in hot oven for 3-4 minutes.

Basic White Sauce

8 fl oz / 250ml milk
1 oz / 30g butter
1 oz / 30g plain flour
salt and pepper

1. Melt the butter and stir in the sifted flour. Cook over low heat for a couple of minutes, until the mixture looks like wet sand.

2. Remove from heat and gradually add the milk, whisking well to blend.

3. Return to heat and bring to simmering point, stirring continuously.

Season with a pinch of salt and pepper. Cook for 4-5 minutes, or until sauce is smooth and coats the back of the spoon.

Sweet Short Pastry

8 oz / 250g plain flour
4 oz / 125g butter (or pastry shortening)
2 teaspoons sifted icing sugar
Pinch of salt
Cold water

1. Sift the flour, icing sugar and salt into a bowl. Add butter or shortening and cut into small pieces, then rub in with fingertips until the mixture resembles breadcrumbs.

2. Add just enough cold water to make the dough hold together.

3. Turn out onto floured work surface and roll out the pastry. Do not handle, knead or roll any more than necessary, or pastry will be tough.

4. To make a fruit or jam tart.

5. Line a greased pie-plate with half the pastry. Fill with cold sweetened stewed fruit or jam.

6. Cover with a layer of pastry, crimp the edges and brush with egg beaten with a little milk. Sprinkle with caster sugar.

7. Bake at 400°F/200°C for about 45 minutes, until crisp and golden brown. Reduce temperature to 350°F/180°C after 15 minutes.

To make a fruit flan.

1. Line a greased flan tin with pastry and trim the edges. Put a piece of baking paper inside the flan and fill with rice or beans (Baking blind).

2. Bake in preheated oven at 400°F/200°C for 15 minutes. Remove paper and rice or beans and leave in oven for another 3 minutes.

3. Remove from oven and allow to cool before filling with fresh or stewed fruit. Glaze with sieved jam or fruit juice thickened with a little gelatine or arrowroot.

I said to her (Marlene Dietrich), with an effort at grey comedy, 'All I demand from my friends nowadays is that they live through lunch,' to which she replied, puzzled, 'Why lunch, sweetheart?'

The Noël Coward Diaries

TEATIME

Noël spent happy holidays with his aunt and uncle in Cornwall. Of a visit in 1915 he writes:

"I was happy by myself in those days, a habit which I mislaid in later years, but have fortunately regained since. I spent many hours wandering along the cliffs, frequently returning drenched to the skin to eat large teas in my aunt's kitchen. Dripping-toast and splits and saffron cake, this last bright yellow and delicious."

Present Indicative

Saffron Cake

1 lb / 500g plain flour
4 oz / 125g butter
½ oz / 11g powdered yeast
¼ teaspoon saffron – threads or powder
3 oz / 85g sugar
½ cup mixed peel
pinch of freshly grated nutmeg
½ teaspoon salt
about 2 tablespoons milk

1. Sift flour into large bowl, cut in butter with blade of knife then rub together with fingertips until mixture resembles breadcrumbs.

2. Add yeast, sugar, mixed peel, salt and spices and mix well.

3. Stir in enough milk to make a stiff dough.

4. Cover and leave to rise for 1 hour.

5. Shape into two round cakes and place on buttered baking sheet, leaving room for cakes to expand.

6. Cut a cross ½"/1cm deep in centre of each cake with a sharp knife and leave to rise for about 1 hour.

7. Place in pre-heated oven and bake at 350°F/180°C for 40-50 minutes, until cakes are golden.

8. Cool on wire racks.

Slice and serve with whipped cream or butter on the day it is made, it is also good toasted the next day.

Some traditional recipes specify lard as the shortening, or half lard, half butter. Lard makes the cake light, butter gives a richer flavour.

Cornish Splits

3/8 oz / 11g powdered yeast – 1 level tablespoon approx. (or ¾ oz / 22g fresh yeast)
½ pint / 250ml milk
1 lb / 450g flour – use strong / bread making flour
1 teaspoon salt
2 oz / 50g oz butter
2 oz / 50g caster sugar

1. Warm milk until blood heat and sprinkle or crumble in yeast – stir until dissolved and leave until mixture bubbles.

2. Sift flour and salt into a large bowl. Add butter, rub in with fingertips.

3. Stir in sugar and milk / yeast mixture. Knead on lightly floured surface until smooth. Return to cleaned bowl, cover with foil or cloth and leave in a warm place to prove until doubled in size (about 1 hour).

4. Turn out and knead again until smooth and elastic. Shape into 1½"/4cm balls.

5. Place gently onto buttered baking sheets. Leave to prove until doubled in size, about 1 hour.

6. Preheat oven to 420°F/210°C. Bake for 15-20 minutes until golden. Remove from baking sheets and place on wire rack. Brush tops with milk.

7. Split and serve warm with butter and/or golden syrup, or allow to cool completely and serve with jam and whipped cream.

Dripping Toast

Cut some thick slices of crusty white bread, toast under very hot grill or better still, over an open fire. Spread generously with good beef dripping. Sprinkle with salt and pepper and a little cayenne if liked. Cut into fingers, place on hot serving dish and keep warm under a cover.

In1913 Noël toured with *Peter Pan*, accompanied by his mother. While playing in Kennington 'Mother invited a lot of the company to tea…. The tea was elaborate, the white Worcester cups (wedding present) were brought out… The tea-party, however, on the whole was considered a great success and the remains of the home-made coffee sponge with walnuts and the Fuller's almond cake brightened our lives for the rest of the week.'

Present Indicative

Coffee Sponge with Walnuts

6 oz / 180g self raising flour
5 oz / 150g caster sugar
4 oz / 125g unsalted butter
pinch of salt
3 eggs
1 tablespoon strong black coffee
milk

1. Butter and line an 8"/20cm cake tin. Pre-heat oven to 375°F/190°C.

2. Cream butter and sugar until light and creamy.

3. Add eggs one at a time, beating well after each one.

4. Stir in dry ingredients and coffee, mix together well. If mixture is too stiff, add a little milk – it should be stiff enough to just hold its shape.

5. Spoon mixture into tin and smooth top.

6. Bake for 1 – 1¼ hours, until cake springs back when pressed lightly in centre.

7. Cool on wire rack. When cool, split in half and sandwich together with coffee butter cream. Ice all over with coffee glace icing and decorate with walnut halves.

To make coffee butter cream:
Beat together 2 oz / 60g softened unsalted butter and 3 oz / 90g sifted icing sugar. Add 1 teaspoon coffee essence or strong coffee. Slowly add small quantity of milk until required spreading consistency is obtained.

To make coffee glace icing:
Place 3-4 tablespoons strong black coffee in a mixing bowl. Add 1 lb/500g sifted icing sugar very slowly, beating constantly with a wooden spoon. If icing is too soft add more icing sugar.
Spread evenly over cake with a palette knife or small spatula dipped in hot water. Decorate with walnut halves while the icing is soft.

(Not Fuller's) Almond Cake

4 eggs, lightly beaten
6 oz / 175g butter
6 oz / 175g castor sugar
6 oz / 175g plain flour
3 oz / 85g almond meal
1 teaspoon baking powder
pinch of salt
¼ teaspoon almond essence
4 oz / 125g whole blanched almonds to decorate

1. Butter a deep 8"/20cm cake tin and line with paper. Pre-heat oven to 325°F/160°C.

2. Cream butter and sugar until pale and fluffy, gradually add the eggs, beating well after each addition.

3. Mix dry ingredients together and fold into the egg mixture, along with almond essence. Mixture should be quite stiff.

4. Spoon mixture into cake tin and smooth top with spatula. Cover top of cake with almonds in desired pattern.

5. Place cake in oven and bake for about 1½ hours. Cover with paper if almonds appear to be getting too brown. Cake is cooked when a metal skewer inserted in centre comes out clean.

6. Leave to cool in tin for 5 minutes then place on wire rack to cool completely.

7. This cake keeps very well, store in an airtight container in a cool place.

'Alfred told me they are making me a chocolate cake for tomorrow.'
This was 'A traditional gesture of Lunt friendship.'

The Noël Coward Diaries

Despite my best efforts the actual recipe has not surfaced, so here's a typical American chocolate cake recipe.

(Possibly) The Lunt's Chocolate Cake

4 oz / 125 g dark chocolate, grated
5 fl oz / 150 ml boiling water
5 fl oz / 150 ml sour milk
2 eggs, well beaten
1 lb / 500g brown sugar
125g butter
1 teaspoon vanilla essence
1 lb / 500g plain flour
1 teaspoon bicarbonate of soda (baking soda)
4 oz / 125g butter, melted

1. Butter and line two 7"/8cm sandwich tins. Pre-heat oven to 350°F/180°C.

2. Dissolve the chocolate in the boiling water.

3. Stir in sugar and melted butter.

4. Add bicarbonate of soda to sour milk and add to chocolate mixture, along with beaten eggs.

5. Add vanilla essence, fold in flour which has been sifted 3 times.

6. Divide evenly between the tins.

7. Bake for 30 - 35 minutes, or until centre of cake springs back when lightly pressed.

8. Cool on cake rack. Join together with chocolate icing and top with Boiled Frosting.

Chocolate Icing

Place 1 oz / 30g softened butter in a bowl, work in 8 oz / 125g icing sugar and a tablespoon cocoa powder. Add a little milk to make a spreadable consistency.

Boiled Frosting

8 oz / 250g sugar
5 fl oz / 125ml boiling water
1 egg white, beaten
few drops of vanilla essence

1. Boil the sugar and water together over high heat until it threads when stirred.

2. Put egg white in a heat proof bowl, pour over the hot syrup and whisk until it has a thick, syrupy consistency.

3. Add vanilla essence.

4. Pour over cake, smooth or swirl with hot, wet palette knife.

'Had hot chocolate and layer cake at Fuller's and a conversation with the waitress, who delivered a tirade against *South Pacific*.'
The Noël Coward Diaries

'…the making of pastry, pies, cakes and soufflés to this day remains a deep mystery, and all these were the things Noël particularly liked to eat.' Cole Lesley describes his cooking ability and Noël's favourite foods.

Here are some favourite old-fashioned layer-cakes.

Caramel Gateau

2 eggs
3 oz / 90g sugar
2 teaspoons cocoa powder
2½ oz / 75g plain flour
salt

1. Butter and line three 6"/15cm sandwich tins.

2. Whisk the eggs and sugar together until frothy.

3. Fold in the sifted flour and salt.

4. Divide into three equal portions, add cocoa powder to one portion.

5. Bake in pre-heated oven at 425°F/220°C for 10 minutes.

6. Allow to cool completely on a cake rack.

7. Sandwich the cakes together, the chocolate one in the middle, with the following butter icing.

2 oz / 60g butter
a tablespoon of cocoa powder
3 oz / 90g icing sugar
about a dessertspoon of milk

Mix all the ingredients together, adding just enough milk to make a spreadable consistency.

Place cake on serving plate. Cover completely with caramel icing, made as follows:

Put 4 oz/125g brown sugar into a saucepan with ¼ cup of water and a pinch of cream of tartar. Boil for 4 minutes. Pour on to a lightly beaten egg white, whisk until thick and creamy. Quickly pour over the cake, smoothing with a wet palette knife. Decorate with chocolate discs. The sides can be covered with chocolate hail, pressed into icing before it is set.

Battenberg Cake

½ lb / 250g butter, softened
1 cup castor sugar
3 eggs
2 cups plain flour
1 teaspoon baking powder
pinch of salt
few drops vanilla essence
milk
cochineal or red food colouring
1 cup raspberry jam
2 cups ground almonds
3 cups pure icing sugar
1 egg, extra
½ teaspoon almond essence
juice of half a lemon

1. Butter and line two deep 7"/18cm square cake tins.

2. Cream the butter and castor sugar together until pale and fluffy.

3. Add eggs, one at a time, beating well after each addition. Add vanilla essence.

4. Stir in sifted flour, baking powder and salt. If mixture seems too stiff add a little milk.

5. Divide mixture in half. Add food colouring to one portion to make it deep pink. Spread the mixture into the prepared tins.

6. Place in pre-heated oven at 350°F/180°C for 25 – 30 minutes, or until a wooden skewer inserted in the centre comes out clean.

7. Remove from oven and leave in tin for 10 minutes, then turn out and cool completely on wire cake rack.

8. Trim the cake edges. Cut each cake lengthwise into 4 equal strips, as wide as the cake is deep. Trim if necessary.

9. Heat the jam slightly and press through a sieve. Spread onto all 4 sides of each strip of cake and join 2 white strips and 2 pink strips together, chequerboard fashion. This recipe will make 2 cakes.

10. Mix together ground almonds, icing sugar, extra egg (beaten), few drops of lemon juice and almond essence.

11. Knead until smooth, adding more lemon juice if it is too dry. Divide into halves.

12. Lightly dust work surface with icing sugar and roll out one portion to about 1/8"/½cm thick. Keep to a rectangular shape large enough to completely wrap around cake.

13. Place cake at one end of almond paste and neatly roll it up, with the join underneath the finished cake. Pinch join together firmly.

14. Cut a trellis pattern on top of cake and decorate with candied violets or rose petals and angelica.

15. Repeat for second cake.

16. Serve cut into thin slices.

Orange Sandwich

2 eggs, beaten
4 oz / 125g butter
4 oz / 125g sugar
4 oz / 125g plain flour
¼ teaspoon baking powder
grated rind of 1 orange

1. Butter and flour two 8"/20cm sandwich tins.

2. Cream butter and sugar together until pale.

3. Add eggs and beat well. Stir in the orange rind.

4. Fold in the sifted flour and baking powder.

5. Divide mixture evenly between tins and place in pre-heated oven 400°F/200°C for 20 minutes, or until cake springs back when lightly touched in centre.

6. Turn out onto wire cake racks and cool.

7. While still slightly warm, sandwich together with orange glacé icing and allow to cool completely.

8. When cold, ice top of cake with orange glacé icing and decorate with segments of crystallised orange before icing has set.

To make orange glacé icing:
Sieve 1 lb/500g icing sugar. Place 3 tablespoons orange juice into a bowl and add the icing sugar, beating well with a wooden spoon to prevent lumps forming.

Hot Chocolate

4 cups milk
2 oz / 60g unsweetened chocolate
2 tablespoons sugar
½ teaspoon vanilla essence
whipped cream

1. Gently heat the milk, chocolate and sugar until the chocolate melts and the sugar has dissolved.

2. Beat with a whisk until foamy, add vanilla essence.

3. Pour into heated mugs or glasses, top with a spoonful of whipped cream.

4. Sprinkle with grated or powdered chocolate.

The chocolate can be replaced by 1½ tablespoons of good quality cocoa mixed with ½ cup boiling water.

Serves 5-6

'Long before I was twelve years old I was capable of buying tickets and counting change...I also found that conversation with casual strangers was stimulating to the imagination. ...It was also a pleasant game to be discovered sobbing wretchedly in the corners of railway carriages or buses in the hope that someone would take pity on me and perhaps give me tea at Fuller's. This was only rarely successful.'

Present Indicative

DINNER

The youthful cast of Charley's Aunt arrived in Chester late on a Sunday afternoon during the spring of 1916 in the middle of a downpour. No accommodation had been arranged.

"We trudged for miles, soaked to the skin…Finally…we found at the end of a lane a nice-looking house with an 'Apartments' board in the window. A flashily-dressed woman opened the door and greeted us with surprising enthusiasm. She …said…dinner was just ready. … Within half an hour (we) were cosily installed in pyjamas and dressing-gowns eating roast mutton and red currant jelly."

Present Indicative

Noël and his colleagues came to realise during the night that the 'Apartment' was actually a brothel. Mr Barth, the company manager, "inevitably found out" and swiftly organised alternative, less comfortable (and no doubt less interesting) accommodation for his charges.

Roast Mutton

A shoulder of mutton – have the butcher remove the skin and bone
Vegetable oil
Salt and pepper

For stuffing:
4 tablespoons breadcrumbs
Salt and pepper
1 egg, lightly beaten
2 teaspoons chopped parsley
½ teaspoon chopped thyme
½ teaspoon chopped rosemary

1. Trim as much fat as possible from meat.

2. Rub meat with salt and pepper and brush both sides liberally with oil.

3. Mix stuffing ingredients together. Spread stuffing over inside of shoulder, roll up and tie with butcher's twine.

4. Put 2 tablespoons oil and ½ cup hot water into heated roasting pan. Place mutton in pan, join downwards.

5. Put into a hot oven (425°F/220°C) for 10 minutes. Lower heat to 350°F/180°C and cook till done, allowing 10 minutes for each pound and 10 minutes over. Allow to rest for at least 15 minutes before carving.

NOTE: It is not easy to get good mutton today. You can substitute lamb – be sure it has a good deep pink colour. Lamb and mutton are best trimmed of as much fat as possible, as it can have a disagreeable flavour and smell. Replace with good quality oil or butter to keep meat succulent. Baste frequently during cooking.

Red Currant Jelly

2½ lbs / 1¼ kg redcurrants
Granulated white sugar
Water

1. Put the redcurrants and enough water to just cover fruit into a preserving pan. Simmer until tender. Mash fruit with wooden spoon or masher and pour into a scalded jelly bag or muslin cloth tied over a clean bucket pr bowl. Leave to drip overnight. Don't squeeze the bag or attempt to speed up the process, or the jelly will be cloudy.

2. Measure the juice and add a cup of sugar for every cup of juice.

3. Put the sugar and juice in a preserving pan and heat until sugar is dissolved, stirring constantly. Skim off any scum.

4. Increase temperature and boil until the jelly reaches setting point. To test, drop a little jelly onto a cold saucer, leave to cool for a minute then gently touch with finger. If a skin has formed which wrinkles, the jelly is ready. Or use a thermometer to check temperature, setting point is 220°F/105°C.

5. Pour into hot, dry jars and seal when cold. Use small jars from, for example, herbs and spices or mustards so the contents can be used in a single sitting. Or spoon the jelly into a pretty serving dish. Store in a cool, dry place.

Good with roast turkey or venison, and, of course, roast mutton.

The archivist at the Savoy Grill, where Noël Coward and friends often dined, was kind enough to send me some facsimile menus from 1949, 1969 and 1971. They are in French, which of course anyone who dined there would be able to read easily. For some reason Lamb Chops is listed in English. There are such delights as 'Le Délice de Turbot Monsieur Roland Culver au Vaudeville ce Soir' and 'Le Parfait Glacé Victoria Palace.'

Monte Carlo, Saturday 6 April 1946. At his hotel Noël gave the Windsors '…a delicious dinner: consommé, marrow on toast, grilled langouste, tournedos with sauce béarnaise, and chocolate soufflé. Poor starving France.'

Present Indicative

Consommé

1 quart / litre good brown stock
8 oz / 50g lean beef
¼ pint / 200ml cold water
white and shell of 1 egg
Bouquet garni (sprig of parsley, bayleaf, 12 peppercorns, strip of lemon rind, blade of mace – tied in muslin)
1 small carrot
small piece of turnip
1 small onion
2 tablespoons sherry
extra small onion, a little butter

1. Finely shred beef and soak in the water.

2. Slice the extra onion and fry in a little butter until black. Drain well, removing as much fat as possible.

3. Cut up the vegetables, place in large pan together with the stock, which has had the fat removed. Add the beef and soaking water, slightly beaten egg white, lightly crushed shell and burnt onion.

4. Stir continually over high heat until boiling. Reduce heat and simmer very gently for 45 minutes.

5. Strain the soup through a cloth. Add the sherry, reheat and serve.

6. A little extra sherry may be added to each serving.

Serves 4 – 5

'I have made a consommé devoutly to be wished.'

Remembered Laughter

Brown Stock

2 lb /1kg shin of beef
8 oz / 250g knuckle of veal
8 oz / 250g bones
8 pints / 4 litres cold water
Bouquet garni
2 teaspoons salt
2 onions
1 carrot
½ turnip
2 sticks celery

1. Cut the meat into pieces, place in large pan with water, bones and salt. Bring to the boil, skim off any scum that rises to the surface.

2. Boil rapidly for 10 minutes, then reduce heat and simmer, covered, for 2 hours.

3. Strain and remove fat before using as required.

Marrow on Toast

Buy some good beef marrow bones already sawn by your butcher into 4"/10cm lengths. Allow one piece of marrow bone per person.

Soak in cold water for at least 12 hours, changing the water several times.

Place in large saucepan and cover with cold, lightly salted water to which you have added a squeeze of lemon juice. Bring to the boil and simmer gently for 30 minutes.

Remove marrow bones and drain well. Scoop out marrow and keep warm.

Toast as many slices of good white bread as required, spread with butter and then the marrow.

Season with a little sea salt and freshly ground black pepper, and a sprinkle of cayenne pepper if liked. Cut the marrow toast into neat shapes. Garnish with small parsley sprigs.

Serve on a hot plate to accompany the consommé. The toast can be eaten on its own or put into the soup.

Tournedos with Sauce Béarnaise

One tournedos for each person, about 1"/2.5cm thick (at least 6 oz /185g each) in one piece, cut from the thickest part of the fillet.

Brush them with melted butter and season with coarsely ground black pepper.

Make your griddle plate or heavy frypan very hot. Put the steaks on and let them sizzle for 2-4 minutes each side. Do not overcook, they must be rare to medium.

Place tournedos on hot serving plate. Serve a bowl of sauce béarnaise on the side.

Sauce Béarnaise

3 egg yolks, beaten
4 oz / 125 g butter, melted
¼ cup white wine
3 tablespoons tarragon vinegar
2 shallots, chopped
6 crushed white peppercorns
lemon juice
salt
a few leaves of tarragon, chopped

1. Put the wine, shallots and peppercorns into a small frying pan over high heat.

2. Let it bubble until reduced to about 3 tablespoons.

3. Strain into the top of a double boiler or a heatproof bowl that will fit over a saucepan tightly. Half fill the bottom saucepan with warm water and place over moderate heat.

4. Add the egg yolks to the reduction, whisk until creamy.

5. Pour in the melted butter, stirring constantly. Season with salt and a few drops of lemon juice.

6. Remove from heat and stir in the tarragon.

7. Unless you are very confident do not attempt to reheat, as it may curdle. Leave in a warm place until required.

It is very important to make sure the sauce doesn't get too hot or too cold.

Chocolate Soufflé

2 tablespoons sugar
2 tablespoons hot water
2 tablespoons butter
2 tablespoons plain flour
¾ cup milk
pinch of salt
1½ oz / 45g unsweetened chocolate
3 egg yolks, beaten until creamy
3 egg whites
extra 3 tablespoons sugar
½ teaspoon vanilla essence
whipped cream to serve

1. Place chocolate in medium sized bowl over hot water. Melt without stirring, the add 2 tablespoons of sugar and the hot water. Stir until smooth.

2. Melt the butter in a small saucepan over gentle heat, stir in the flour and salt.

3. Gradually add milk, stirring continuously until mixture reaches boiling point. Add to the chocolate mixture.

4. Add the egg yolks and beat well. Set mixture aside to cool.

5. Pre-heat oven to 350°F/180°C.

6. Beat the egg whites until stiff, beat in the 3 tablespoons sugar, a little at a time. Stir in the vanilla essence.

7. Take a tablespoon of the egg whites and stir into the chocolate mixture, then fold in the rest of the egg whites.

8. Pour into prepared 8"/20cm soufflé dish.

9. Bake for 25 minutes. Soufflé will have a crusty top and be slightly creamy in the centre. If you want it even textured bake for an extra 10 minutes.

10. Serve immediately, accompanied by a bowl of lightly whipped cream.

Serves 4 – 5.

NOTE: Soufflé can be prepared up to step 4 well in advance

To prepare a soufflé mould or dish:

Cut a double band of heavy paper (baking paper is good) 1"/2½cm deeper than the mould or dish. Wrap around the outside of the container and pin or tape in place.

When the soufflé is set or cooked remove paper, using a knife to ease it away from the soufflé.

'Dinner tonight was the *coup de grâce*; shrimps à la Créole, corn, peas, pimentoes, custard pie tartlets and a series of explosions of wind that are still continuing as I write.' Noël is describing Alfred's exquisite cooking, in a letter to Cole Lesley written during an idyllic holiday with the Lunts.

Shrimps à la Créole

1 lb / 500g cooked shrimps
1 onion, chopped
1 green capsicum, finely chopped
1 oz / 30g butter
2 large tomatoes, peeled and chopped
½ cup sliced mushrooms
½ cup dry sherry
1½ cups water or stock
salt and pepper

1. Melt the butter in a saucepan and sauté the onion and capsicum until soft.

2. Add the tomatoes and mushroom, cook for about 2 minutes.

3. Add the water or stock, heat to boiling point. Add sherry and season to taste with salt and pepper.

4. Serve shrimps on a bed of steamed rice, pour sauce over.

Serves 4

Custard Pie Tartlets

Filling:
4 eggs, well beaten
4 oz / 125g sugar
pinch of salt
½ teaspoon vanilla essence
3½ cups milk
freshly grated nutmeg

1. Mix all the ingredients except the nutmeg together, stir until sugar is dissolved.

2. Pour into prepared tart shells and sprinkle with nutmeg.

3. Bak in pre-heated oven at 425ºF/220ºC for 10 minutes. Reduce heat to 300ºF/150ºC and bake for another 10 to 15 minutes, or until firm.

4. Cool on wire cake rack. Serve warm or chilled.

Makes 12 tartlets.

Tart Shells

1½ cups plain flour
pinch of salt
1 teaspoon caster sugar
4 oz / 125g butter
½ cup cold water

1. Combine flour, salt and sugar in bowl and mix well. Cut the butter into the dry ingredients and, using your fingertips, quickly work the mixture together until it resembles breadcrumbs.

2. Add about half of the water, mixing with a flat knife or your fingers, continue adding water slowly until the dough holds together.

3. Press dough into a ball, wrap in cling film and refrigerate for 15 minutes.

4. Grease 12 x 4"/10cm tart plates.

5. Roll out pastry to about ¼ / ½cm thick. Line the tart plates and prick bases with a fork.

'Many first nighters complained that the dinner scene was the longest meal they had ever sat through.' Noël, referring to *This Was a Man*.

(The meal is preceded by cocktails. It starts with caviar, followed by soup, partridges and attendant vegetables, pêche Melba, coffee and liqueurs. All the courses are accompanied by champagne.)

COOKING WITH NÖEL

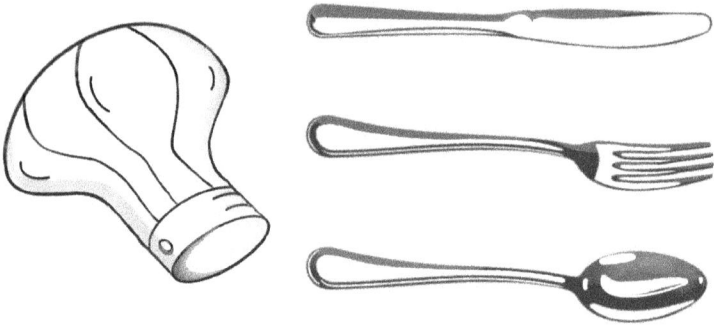

Noël, in Bermuda in 1956 with Graham and Coley, was hit by a 'cooking craze.'

'A cook was not to be had for love or the large amount of money we offered…'

'I have taken to cooking and listening to Wagner, both of which frighten me to death.'

'We have been having great fun cooking…our kitchen scenes are good sound slapstick comedy…'

'I have so far made, unaided, pancakes, a chocolate cake, a coffee mousse, a crab mousse, and…Yorkshire pudding.'

The Noël Coward Diaries

Pancakes

8 oz / 125g plain flour
2 eggs
¼ cup sugar
pinch of salt
1 pint / 600ml milk
melted butter for frying
lemon juice and castor sugar to serve

1. Break the eggs into a bowl, add the salt and sugar and whisk gently.

2. Starting with the flour, add the flour and milk alternately, a little at a time, beating until well blended.

3. The batter should be smooth and have the consistency of cream. Pour into a jug. Leave to stand for at least 10 minutes, but no longer than 1 hour.

4. Heat a heavy based omelette pan and brush the base with melted butter.

5. When really hot, pour in some batter and tilt the pan so it covers the bottom evenly.

6. When the surface is cooked and dry – in a few seconds – flip it over with a sharp jerk upwards and slightly away from you. If you feel that is beyond you, turn with a palette knife.

7. Cook the second side for about 30 seconds, slide out onto a warmed plate.

8. Sprinkle with lemon juice and castor sugar, roll up or fold into quarters and keep warm while you make the rest of the pancakes.

Makes about 10 pancakes.

The pancakes can also be filled with jam or stewed fruit.
They can be stacked if preferred, with the filling spread between them, then cut into wedges to serve.

Chocolate Cake

6 oz / 200g plain flour
1 tablespoon cocoa powder
1 teaspoon baking powder
4 oz / 125g butter
few drops vanilla essence
4 oz / 125g sugar
2 eggs
pinch of salt
about ¼ cup milk

1. Butter and line a 6"/15cm cake tin.

2. Cream the butter and sugar until pale and fluffy.

3. Add the eggs one at a time, beating well after each one.

4. Stir in the sifted flour, cocoa, baking powder and salt.

5. Add the vanilla essence and enough milk to make a soft dropping consistency.

6. Turn mixture into prepared tin and bake in a pre-heated oven at 350°F/180°C for 45-60 minutes, until cake springs back when gently touched in centre.

7. Turn onto cake rack and cool completely before icing all over with chocolate butter icing.

Chocolate Butter Icing

2 oz / 60g butter
3 oz / 90g icing sugar
2 teaspoons of milk
2 teaspoons of cocoa powder
few drops of vanilla essence

1. Sift icing sugar and cocoa into a basin, add softened butter and beat together until creamy.

2. Add vanilla essence. Beat in just enough milk to make a spreading consistency.

NOTE: To add some excitement the vanilla essence can be replaced by peppermint essence.

'…maybe the day will come when I can cook a joint, stuff a chicken's arse with butter, and make pastry so light that it flies away at a touch. My solo triumphs to date have been a chocolate mousse (plus cinnamon, Nescafe and Crème de Cacao) some rather curiously shaped croquettes, Kitchener eggs, sensational salad dressing with bacon rinds, various experimental soups originating from tins but rising to ambrosial height after my pudgy fingers have been busy with herbs and garlic, and last but by no means least a coquille of shrimps and smoked oysters.'

The Noël Coward Diaries

Coffee Mousse

10 fl oz / 300ml cream
2 egg yolks, lightly beaten
2 egg whites, stiffly beaten
½ cup strong coffee, cold
2 oz / 60g sugar
1 oz / 30g gelatine

1. Put the coffee and sugar into a saucepan. Heat until warm then sprinkle gelatine over, stir over low heat until completely dissolved.

2. Remove from heat, allow to cool a little and add cream.

3. Pour onto egg yolks and beat well.

4. Fold in the stiffly beaten egg whites.

5. Pour into a soufflé dish and chill until set.

Serves 4.

Crab Mousse

12 oz / 750g crab meat – fresh, frozen or tinned
1 teaspoon gelatine
2 egg whites, stiffly beaten
1 tablespoon butter
1 tablespoon plain flour
½ pint / 300ml fish stock or half milk, half water
¼ cup cream
salt and ground white pepper

1. Make a white sauce by melting the butter in a saucepan over moderate heat, then stirring in the flour and cooking until it looks like wet sand.

2. Gradually add the stock or milk and water, stirring continually with a wooden spoon until thickened.

3. Sprinkle the gelatine over the hot white sauce and stir until completely dissolved.

4. Flake the crab and remove any bits of shell or hard pieces. Stir into the white sauce and season to taste.

5. Stir in the cream, then thoroughly fold in the stiffly beaten egg whites.

6. Pour into a wet mould and chill for about 2 hours before serving.

Serves 2 – 3 as a light luncheon dish with salad and bread.

Yorkshire Pudding

6 oz / 185g sifted plain flour
2 eggs
salt and pepper
6 fl oz / 185ml milk
4 fl oz / 125ml water

1. Make well in flour, beat in eggs then add liquid, whisk well until smooth. Can be prepared ahead of time and left to stand.

2. Heat 2 tablespoons fat in baking tin (11" x 9" / 25cm x 23cm) until smoking hot. Pour in batter, place in hot oven (425°F/220°C) for 25-35 minutes.

3. Drain off any excess fat before cutting into squares to serve. Serve very hot with roast beef and gravy.

Serves 6 – 8

'A most unexpected sideline to Noël's culinary activities was that he genuinely loved to do the washing-up. He didn't want to help to dry, he wanted to plunge his arms up to the elbows in the greasy suds, and scour the pots and pans until they were all shining bright and clinically clean.'

Remembered Laughter

'I am inclined to put in far too much flavouring, as in painting I put in far too much colour, but I am learning restraint.'

'I am … learning to be fearless with eggs and undismayed by deep fat and flour and breadcrumbs. It all comes under the heading of living dangerously…'

Noël Coward at Firefly, his home in Jamaica. 'I am sick of too many people at meals. Last night was bliss. I dined alone up here – steak and onions and sweet potatoes in a puree whipped up by me. I gave myself a gin and tonic and a Spanish lesson, retired to bed at 9.30 and read an extremely good biography of James I and slept like a top.'

The Noël Coward Diaries

FOREIGN FOOD'S THE THING

Amanda: Do you know, I really think I love travelling more than anything else in the world! ...the most thrilling thing of all, arriving at strange places, and seeing strange people, and eating strange foods ----
Elyot: And making strange noises afterwards.

Private Lives

'Well, the holiday (in Avallon) started with a bang ...when the back axle broke in half (on the Jaguar).... Yesterday was further complicated by Little Lad having an appalling attack of wind after eating Lobster Gateau at Barbizon, made with such a lot of cream and washed down with vin rose,'

Rembered Laughter

It was probably Lobster Galettes, traditionally layered like a gateau, that caused Graham's distress. They are delicious but very rich.

Lobster Galettes

For 4 galettes

1 large lobster, freshly cooked
4 fl oz / 125ml white wine
2 oz / 60g butter
juice of a lemon
4 fl oz / 12ml fish stock or water
8 fl oz / 250ml thick cream
sea salt and freshly ground black pepper
white part of 3 spring onions, finely sliced
4 galettes, warmed
lemon wedges and parsley or fennel, to garnish

1. Remove all flesh from lobster and cut into chunks.

2. Heat butter in frying pan and gently cook the spring onions until soft but not brown.

3. Add white wine, stock or water, increase heat and simmer until liquid is reduced by half.

4. Add cream and simmer very gently until thick. Remove from heat.

5. Fold in the lobster flesh and reheat gently. Add salt and pepper to taste.

6. Place a galette on a warmed plate, spread one-third of the mixture over, then continue in layers. Cut into wedges to serve. Or fill each galette, then fold in half or turn in edges all round.

7. Garnish with lemon wedges and parsley or fennel sprigs.

Galettes

For 8 galettes
8½ oz / 250g buckwheat flour
1 egg
1 teaspoon coarse sea salt
3½ fl oz / 100ml milk
butter or lard for cooking the galettes

Make the batter in advance. Sift the flour into a mixing bowl and make a well in the centre. Put the egg and salt into the well and mix with your hands or a wooden spoon, gradually drawing in the flour. Mix the milk with 7 fl oz/200ml of water and add the liquid a little at a time to the mixture until the batter is smooth and has the consistency of thick mayonnaise.

Traditionally, you should now beat the batter energetically for at least 15 minutes, slapping it from side to side of the mixing bowl; but it is simpler to put it in a food processor and work it for 7-8 minutes, until very smooth. With the motor running, mix in more of the milk and water mixture until the batter has the consistency of thin cream. Leave it to rest in a cool place for at least 2 hours, or preferably overnight.

Preheat the oven to 230°F/110°C. Generously grease a 10"/25cm frying pan with butter or lard and place over a medium heat. Give the batter a good stir, then put a ladleful into the hot frying pan and swirl it around so that the batter spreads all over the surface. Cook until the edges begin to brown, then carefully turn the galette over and cook until it is slightly crisply.
Stack the galettes as you make them with a piece of foil between them to prevent them from sticking together, and keep them warm in the oven.
(From Brittainy gastronomique by Kate Whiteman)

Noël loved to travel, as everyone who has read his biographies and diaries will know. Graham Payn says 'The love of spices must have originated on those early oriental journeys…'

Noël recalls '…a fabulous Arab meal (in Marrakech). We sat on cushions …and ate, with our fingers, a dish called pastillia. This was a sort of flat, covered pancake made of chiffon-thin pastry with sugar on top and partridges, bacon, herbs, etc., inside. Then a delicious dish was brought in under an enormous straw hat, which was baby chickens done with lemon and spices. …We all got in rather a mess but it was worth it. One of the most entirely satisfactory meals I have had anywhere.'

Present Indicative

This pigeon pie is a close match for the pastillia.

Pigeon Pie

3 x 400g (14 oz) squab pigeons or spring chickens
4 sprigs each fresh parsley and coriander, tied into a bunch
1 stick cinnamon
½ teaspoon black pepper
A good pinch of sea salt
1 onion, peeled and grated
200g (7 oz) unsalted butter
200g (7 oz) whole blanched almonds
Ground cinnamon
2 tablespoons icing sugar
4 whole eggs
Yolks of 4 eggs
500g (1 lb) filo pastry

Place the pigeons breast side down in a heavy pan in which they will just fit. Add the herbs, cinnamon, pepper, salt, grated onion and 60g (2½ oz) of butter. Bring to the boil, turn down to a slow simmer, cover and leave to cook for 1¼ hours.

Gently fry the whole almonds in 25g (1 oz) of butter until golden brown. When the almonds are cool grind them coarsely. Sift together 1 teaspoon ground cinnamon and two thirds of the icing sugar and mix thoroughly into the almonds.

Remove the cooked pigeons from the pan and leave to cool. Reduce the poaching liquid t half its volume then leave to cool. Beat the eggs and yolks until they are frothy. Stir the beaten eggs into the broth. Return the pan to the lowest heat and stir constantly for 5 minutes, until the mixture thickens to produce a thick sauce. Check the seasoning.

Remove the skin form the birds and with your fingers shred the flesh, discarding all the bones. Preheat the oven to 180°C/350°F/ gas mark 4.

Melt the remaining butter over a low heat and skim off the scum. Lightly grease a non-stick shallow round pie tin. Lay a sheet of filo across it, letting the edges hang over, and brush lightly with melted butter. Lay another sheet at a 60° angle and again brush the surface with butter. Repeat with another 4 sheets of filo, until the surface of the pie dish is completely covered and the circle is complete.

Scatter the shredded pigeon over the pastry and top with the egg sauce. Fold two layers of filo in half and place in the preheated oven for 1 minute, to crisp up. Place these over the egg sauce and top with the almond, cinnamon and sugar mixture. Fold in the overlapping edges of filo, brushing the surface lightly with butter. Now lay two sheets of filo over the surface and gently tuck them under the base, cutting off any excess. Brush the surface with melted butter and pour remaining butter around the edges of the tin.

Bake in the preheated oven for 30 minutes then carefully invert the pie onto a baking sheet. Bake it upside down for a further 20 minutes, Return to top side up. Bake for a further 10 minutes until the top is crispy golden. Sprinkle the surface with cinnamon and icing sugar and serve absolutely piping hot.

Tagine of Chicken with preserved lemon

1.35 - 1.5kg (2½ –3½ lb) chicken
3 cloves garlic, peeled and crushed
1 teaspoon coarse sea salt
Stalks from a small bunch fresh coriander, very finely chopped
(Reserve the coriander leaves)
Juice of ½ lemon
1 large white onion, peeled and grated
1 teaspoon freshly
ground black pepper
1 teaspoon ground ginger
¼ teaspoon saffron filaments
4 tablespoons olive oil
1 stick cinnamon
2 preserved lemons
175g (6 oz) green cracked olives
Coriander leaves

Rub the garlic, salt, lemon juice and coriander stalks into the cavity of the chicken. Mix together the onion, spices and olive oil and rub over the outside of the chicken. Leave to stand for 30 minutes.

Place the chicken breast-side down in a tagine or heavy oval casserole, making sure you add all the marinade juices. Pour in sufficient water to cover two thirds of the chicken and add the stick of cinnamon. Bring the water to the boil, then reduce to a simmer and cook for 1 hour, turning the chicken several times during cooking. Preheat the oven to 150°C/300°F gas mark 2.

Rinse the preserved lemons and olives under cold running water. Remove flesh from the preserved lemons and cut into strips. Remove the chicken from the casserole, place in an earthenware serving dish and cover with foil to keep warm (if you have a tagine, drain the sauce into a pan). Turn up the heat under the casserole for 5 minutes to reduce the sauce. Pour the sauce over the chicken in the tagine.

Add the olives and preserved lemons. Garnish with coriander leaves.

Preserved Lemon

2kg (4½ lb) lemons, unwaxed
200g (7 oz) coarse sea salt

Quarter the lemons from the top to within 1 cm (½") from the bottom, so that the lemons remain attached at one end. Sprinkle plenty of salt onto the cut flesh then press them back into shape.

Place some salt on the base of a sterilized preserving jar just big enough to hold the lemons. Pack in the lemons, sprinkling with salt as you go. Add the remaining salt and press down on the lemons to release their juices – there should be enough juice to cover the surface. If not, top up with additional fresh lemon juice.

Leave for at least a month before using.

'In all my travels I have endured discomfort fairly cheerfully when I have had to, but I never have sought it out. … I have a Ritz mind and always have had. To hell with local colour!'

The meals he endured on his journeys were often less than Ritz-standard.

In the Seychelles, 'The food…is indescribable. I don't think in all my journeyings I have ever encountered worse. The butter is always rancid and what they do to the meat and fish is macabre.'

Marrakech – in a letter to Cole. 'We had Arab food, cous-cous etc: in fact damp mutton but vurry atmospheric deerr. The food in this hotel is lethal. I was served last night with a black rubber turd which was laughingly listed on the menu as steak au poivre. I sent it back with a flea in its ear.'

Remembered Laughter

In America he experienced a clambake. 'Elaborate preparations: chickens, lobsters, corn, clams, etc., etc., were buried in the sand under seaweed and cooked for hours and hours. …Nothing was cooked enough and everything was full of sand. …The white wine was delicious provided you waited until the sand had sunk to the bottom of the mug. Finally we all came indoors and had some milk and angel cake, the lack of sand in which was somehow shocking.'

The Noël Coward Diaries

'The dining room of the Astoria Hotel (in Leningrad) was cool and dim and the tablecloths were filthy. I asked for caviar … it was large and grey and delicious. The chicken that followed was also large and grey, but less delicious.'

Future Indefinite

'Noël and Graham became fond of Violet (Ian Fleming's cook/housekeeper at Goldeneye) in spite of her cuisine;'

'…the delicious dinners became a monotonous succession of either salt fish and ackee or curried goat followed by stewed guavas with coconut cream, all of them tasting of armpits and so dreaded by Noël that he used to cross himself before each morsel.'

Remembered Laughter

These traditional Jamaican recipes are delicious and worth trying, it must have been the too frequent appearance or indifferent cooking that provoked such a violent response. They are inspired by recipes in *Down to Earth Jamaican Cooking* by Laurice de Gale

Ackee and Salted Codfish

½ lb / 250g salted codfish
2 cans ackee, drained
½ cup cooking oil
1 medium-sized onion, finely chopped
1 medium-sized tomato, chopped
1 red chilli (seeds removed and roughly chopped)
Black pepper
¼ teaspoon thyme leaves

1. Cook the codfish in water for 15 minutes, drain.

2. Rinse the fish in cold water to cool. Flake and set aside, feeling for and removing any bones.

3. Wash the ackee in a colander with hot water to remove the brine, set aside.

4. Heat the oil in a frying pan.

5. Add the onions, tomato, chilli and thyme. Sauté until the onions are tender.

6. Add the ackee and fish and mix gently together.

7. Sprinkle with black pepper.

8. Serve hot. Makes 4 – 6 servings.

Curried Goat

2 lbs / 1kg goat meat
1 teaspoon salt
½ teaspoon black pepper
3 tablespoons good quality curry powder
2 cloves garlic, finely chopped
1 onion, finely chopped
1 spring onion, chopped
2 bay leaves
1 small red chilli, chopped (with or without seeds)
2 sprigs thyme or ½ teaspoon dried thyme
2½ cups water

1. Wash and cut the meat into bite-sized pieces.

2. Combine seasoning ingredients and rub into the meat.

3. Cover and leave to marinate overnight or for at least 4 hours.

4. Bring the water to boil in a heavy saucepan. Add the goat meat, the seasonings and the marinade, stir.

5. Cover the pot and cook slowly over medium heat, stir occasionally.

6. Continue to simmer for at least 1-2 hours or until the meat is tender and easily separates from the bones. Add more water if necessary.

7. Taste and correct the seasoning. If the gravy is too thin, increase heat and reduce the liquid to desired consistency or add a small amount of freshly grated breadcrumbs. Remove bay leaves before serving.

Serve on top of piping hot boiled rice. A fresh green salad is a good accompaniment.

Makes 4 – 6 servings.

Amanda: Did you eat sharks' fins, and take your shoes off, and use chopsticks and everything?
Elyot: Practically everything.

Amanda: There's no doubt about it, foreign travel's the thing.

Private Lives

ON DIETING, HEALTH & APPEARANCE

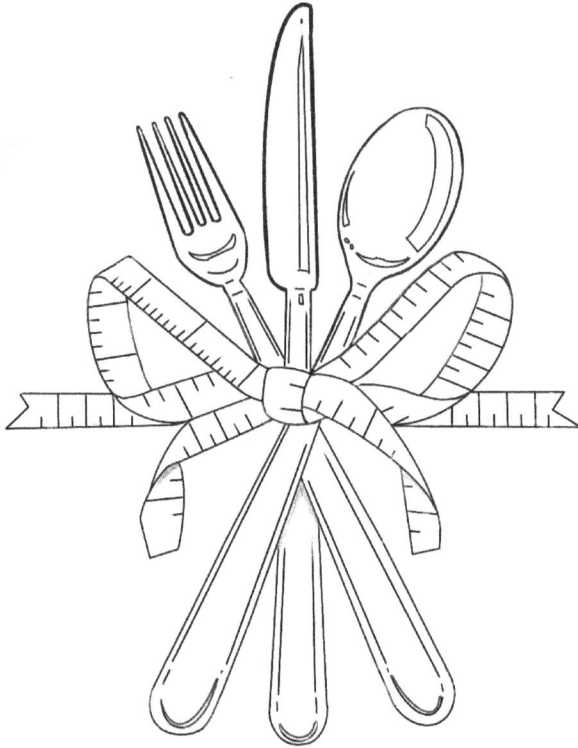

'…my two weaknesses are my colon and my feet!'

The Noël Coward Diaries

Throughout his life Noël was to spend a considerable amount of time in hospitals, clinics and nursing homes. He was prone to severe digestive disorders, stomach and circulatory problems, probably aggravated by his often unwise diet and the pace at which he lived and worked. Today his ailments would be diagnosed as stress related.

When he had to undergo 'a minor operation', two days before rehearsals for *This Year of Grace* were due to begin, although 'in bad pain and a worse temper,' Noël's memory of his time in the nursing home is of an escape from the pressures of the world.

'There was …a pleasant sense of timelessness. … A gentle dimness enveloped me, a detachment from affairs. The life outside seemed incredibly remote. …I could relax, comfortably aware…that I should be up and about again before this delicious enforced rest had had time to become tedious.'

Noël knew he was risking his health by pushing himself too hard. In a letter to Cole Lesley, written from his suite at the Dorchester where he was confined to bed with pneumonia, 'I had a curious feeling …that the pace was getting too hot. …I was beginning to get frantic and panic-stricken. The Almighty…when he observes me going too far, …firmly knocks me out. I am most grateful to him.'

At La Source, Lausanne, he underwent tests for unexplained severe abdominal pain. 'The food is ghastly. And the times of serving it barbaric. To have to face a badly cooked steak swimming in unutterable gravy at 11.30 a.m. is a lot to expect. I'm constantly sending things back and stuffing myself with sugar and eggs and cream, but it's all pretty difficult with incessant gut pains and no appetite.'

'A violent week and now I am going into hospital for three days to get a real proper check-up.' But the food served at the hospital in Chicago was not to his liking. '…a grey woman arrived with a menu. I chose and marked devilled-egg salad, cheese, rye bread, French dressing and iced tea. An hour or so later a tray was brought me on which was a cup of vegetable soup, a pear in a bed of lettuce with mayonnaise, a hunk of hamburger covered in ketchup accompanied by two moist boiled potatoes, a corn on the cob which I didn't attempt on account of my teeth, and a pistachio ice-cream which tasted like brilliantine. I ate very little of all this ambrosia, but enjoyed the coffee which came instead of the iced tea.'

During the same visit, '... when the tray finally arrived the eggs were lying sullenly in the water they'd been poached in, which was not very appetizing.'

Ever conscious of his public image, Noël kept an eye on his weight and often dieted. He also frequently resolved to give up drinking for his health and his figure's sake.

Cole Lesley records, 'The fact must be faced that ... (before beginning rehearsals for *Present Laughter*) Noël had been eating far too many rich French meals, the entrees blanketed with sauces and the puddings smothered with cream. For the first time in his life he lost the lean and elegant figure for which he had been so famous and was furious when he ultimately saw the photographs of himself in Leslie Benson's (pink) dressing-gown; how could Graham and I let him appear looking like a vast pink sausage?'

In 1956 a diary entry reads. '...Health and happiness are more important than lissomness...Be your age and be your weight and conserve your vitality by eating enough and enjoying it...I need sweets and starch and alcohol in moderation because I enjoy them, and I am damned if I am going to upset my metabolism and thereby my health and happiness by straining after a youthful line that is gone for ever.'

A few years later.' I drink two glasses of skim milk per day (tidged up with vanilla and sweetening), two eggs for my lunch, and steak and sliced tomato for my dinner. For breakfast only fruit juice and coffee. It is monotonous, of course, but the effect is sensational.'

Jamaica, 1949 'Made a vow to give up drinking. I don't need it, I don't particularly like it, it is fattening and boring, and so no more of it.'

A month later. 'Lunched…Too many martinis. Slept in the afternoon. More martinis.'

'The only trouble about not drinking is that other people who are drinking are liable to look a little silly.'

'What is wrong is my diet. I must eat more raw foods – fruit and vegetables – and alcohol is definitely bad for me. I shall therefore not drink – I couldn't mind less.'

COCKTAILS & MORE

Florence: 'It's never too early for a cocktail.'

The Vortex

Cole Lesley in *Remembered Laughter* writes that during one Jamaican winter '… at (Mrs Churchill's) request we initiated her into the pleasures of Jamaican rum punch. This she found so delicious – ice-cold on a tropical evening – that she quickly asked for more and as quickly finished it, Noël and I (were) a little worried, though we need not have been; the only result was a merry party.'

Jamaican Rum Punch

1 cup lime juice
1 cup sugar syrup
2 cups white rum
4 cups water or diluted fruit juice
a few pimentos (all-spice)

Mix all ingredients together, leave as long as possible for flavours to blend. Serve over crushed ice.

Another local recipe.

Jamaican Planter's Punch

4 tablespoons sugar
4 tablespoons water
10 tablespoons rum
dash of lime juice
2 slices pineapple

Mix first four ingredients together and stir until sugar has dissolved.

Add pineapple, finely chopped.

Serve over crushed ice, garnish with cherries and mint leaves.

'We… introduced the Queen Mother to Bullshots, she had two and was delighted.'

The Noël Coward Diaries

Bullshot

2½ oz vodka
5 oz beef bouillon
dash Worcestershire sauce

dash of bitters
dash of Tabasco

Shake with crushed ice, strain into red wine glass or tumbler. Garnish with twist of lemon.

Old Man's Thing

'Hey for the blowfish, blowfish,
Ho for the wedding ring
Hey for the Dry Martinis, old goat fricassee, Old Man's Thing.'

(Part of a calypso composed by Noël on the marriage of his neighbour Ian Fleming and Ann Rothermere in Jamaica.)

'A crockery punchbowl was fetched from the kitchen, into which Ian peeled an orange and a lime (or a lemon will do), never failing to peel the rind in one long spiral; a point of honour with him. Then over these two whorls he poured a bottle of crude white rum of appalling potency and, in the dark, set the whole thing alight to cheers from the company. When the flames died down we drank the strong concoction with many toasts to their happiness'.

In *Bitter-Sweet* a song is dedicated to

> 'Tokay! The golden sunshine of a summer day.
> ...Tokay! Will bear the burden of your cares away.'

Many famous people were entertained at Goldenhurst. Cole Lesley writes that just before Mr and Mrs Eden were due to arrive one weekend, 'We found to our horror that Mrs Coward had gone on buying the same white wine Mr Coward discovered some years before during an economy drive. It was labelled a Sauterne Type and cost 2/9 a bottle...We rectified this but then went too far in the other direction and bought a bottle of good port to be handed round, after the pudding and a savoury, with dessert. This was a dead failure, refused by everybody;'

Graham Payn remembers 'before lunch there'd be a gin and tonic, before dinner a dry martini. In later years, he would nurse a diluted brandy-and-ginger.'

In Noël Coward's plays, the characters frequently quaff champagne and cocktails. In the introduction to *Play Parade* (1933), he writes '…for many years I was seldom mentioned in the press without allusions to "cocktails", "post-war hysteria", and "decadence". '

Highballs are often mixed and drunk during the plays – these are traditional 'long' drinks, made with a nip of brandy, gin, rum or whisky poured over ice in a tumbler. Top up with the mixer of choice – soda, dry ginger or tonic – and garnish with a slice of lemon.

One of the most memorable cocktail moments occurs in *Private Lives*, when Elyot and Amanda both step onto the terrace carrying two champagne cocktails each.

Champagne Cocktails

Place a sugar cube in each glass, preferably a champagne saucer. Sprinkle each cube with a few drops of bitters, pour over a nip of brandy. Top up with chilled champagne.

Felicity: She seemed quite at ease to me, sitting there sipping away at that disgusting lemonade. Why couldn't she have a nice healthy Martini like everyone else?

Relative Values

Dry Martini

2 oz gin
¼ oz dry (French) vermouth
Shake with ice and strain into martini glass. Garnish with twist of lemon peel or a green olive.

Sweet Martini

2 oz gin
½ oz sweet (Italian) vermouth
Shake with ice and strain into martini glass. Garnish with a twist of orange peel or a cherry.

Cavalcade opens with preparations to celebrate a new year and a new century. Bridges, the butler, enters with a bottle of champagne in a bucket of ice.

Ellen (the parlourmaid): They won't need champagne if they've got 'ot punch, will they?
Bridges: You never know; best to be on the safe side.

Hot Rum Punch

1 bottle red wine
juice and grated zest of 1 lemon
½ cup brandy
1 stick of cinnamon
½ teaspoon whole allspice

Simmer together for 5 minutes. Strain into warmed punch bowl and add 1½ cups dark rum. Put a slice of lemon into each glass before adding hot punch.

Jennifer: Would you like something to drink? Maria's been awfully clever lately with lemons and oranges and cloves and soda water all mixed up. It sounds filthy but it isn't really."

The Young Idea

Maria's (or my) Fruit Punch

4 oranges
2 lemons
6 oz / 200 g sugar
1 cup unsweetened pineapple juice
1 pint / 600ml unsweetened dark grape juice
a pinch of ground cloves and freshly grated nutmeg
pinch of salt
a few mint sprigs
soda water and ice to serve

1. Rub the sugar into the orange and lemon peel until it is yellow.

2. Place in glass bowl with the pineapple juice.

3. Squeeze the oranges and lemons, add to the pineapple juice along with salt, spices and mint.

4. Stir well and leave to stand for a couple of hours. Strain before using.

5. Pour over crushed ice and add soda water to taste.

Leo: Better have some more Sherry.
Otto: I'm afraid it isn't very good Sherry.
Leo (*scrutinizing the bottle*): It ought to be good; it's real old Armadildo.
Otto: Perhaps we haven't given it a fair chance.

Design for Living

THINGS TO HAVE WITH DRINKS

'Leave the canapés to me.'

Graham Payn in *My Life with Noël Coward* describes *Huîtres Surprises a la Noël*, Noël's own invention. They were tinned oysters coated with mashed potato and deep-fried; Noël proudly served them at a drinks party for the locals in Bermuda.

'Nobody said a word, … Noël was, frankly, rather hurt. … Admittedly, he hadn't expected the grey colour to seep through quite so much. …As we tidied up, all was revealed. In every plant pot, behind every piece of furniture, was a grey virgin huître.'

This version may have been more acceptable.

Oyster Patties

Coat oysters (fresh or bottled) with flour seasoned with a little salt and cayenne pepper. Dip in beaten egg then in dry breadcrumbs.

For 24 oysters, heat 2 oz /60g butter and 2 tablespoons olive oil in heavy based pan. When sizzling hot, add oysters and fry for about two minutes, then turn over and fry for another minute.
Drain on kitchen paper, keep warm until ready to serve. Garnish with lemon and a grind of black pepper.

'The *bouquet* to celebrate the completion of the new roof (at Les Avants) was a great success. A trestle table loaded with bottles of wine and cheese tartlets.'

My Life with Noël Coward

Cheese Tartlets

20 cooked puff pastry tart shells or vol-au-vent cases
4 oz / 125g grated cheddar or Gruyere cheese
1 egg, beaten
¼ cup cream
¼ cup fresh breadcrumbs
½ teaspoon prepared mustard
1 oz / 30 g butter
salt and pepper
grated parmesan cheese

1. Mix together the egg, breadcrumbs and cream.

2. Melt the butter and stir in the grated cheese.

3. Add all other ingredients and stir over very gentle heat until mixture is smooth.

4. Spoon into prepared tart cases. Sprinkle with grated parmesan.

5. Bake in pre-heated oven at 350°F/180°C for about 10 minutes, until golden brown.

In *Design for Living* Gilda offers Otto a glass of Sherry, or something stronger. He replies, 'No, Sherry's all right. It's gentle and refined, and imparts a discreet glow. Of course, I'm used to having biscuits with it.'

When I asked selected aficionados of sherry what biscuits should be served with it, I received a different answer from each person. To avoid any hurt feelings, I offer them all.

Ratafias

2 egg whites
8 oz / 250 g castor sugar
¼ teaspoon almond essence
7 oz / 225g almond meal (finely ground)

1. Whisk the egg whites until frothy. Add the sugar, almond essence and almond meal.

2. Roll mixture into very small balls.

3. Place on well greased baking trays (or tray lined with baking paper), leaving room to spread out. Place in pre-heated oven at 350°F/180°C.

4. Bake for 10 minutes or until the biscuits feel very firm to touch.

5. Cool on a wire rack and store in an airtight container.

Makes about 80 tiny biscuits.

Rout Biscuits

4 oz / 110g castor sugar
4 oz / 110g almond meal (finely ground)
1 egg yolk
a few drops of almond essence

1. Mix all the ingredients together.

2. Roll into small balls, place on well-greased baking tray (or tray lined with baking paper).

3. Brush with beaten egg white.

4. Bake in pre-heated oven at 400°F/ 200°C for about 5 minutes.

5. Cool on wire rack and store in an airtight container.

Makes about 50 biscuits.

Lady Fingers

3 egg whites
2 oz / 60 g icing sugar
2 egg yolks
½ teaspoon vanilla essence
pinch of salt
1½ oz / 45g plain flour

1. Butter lady finger tins or line a baking sheet with baking paper.

2. Beat the egg whites until soft peaks form, then beat in the icing sugar.

3. Beat together the egg yolks, vanilla essence and salt until pale and creamy.

4. Fold the flour into the egg yolk mixture, then gently but thoroughly fold in the egg whites.

5. Spoon into the tins, or, using a pastry bag fitted with plain ½"/ 2½cm nozzle, pipe 2"/5cm lengths onto baking paper.

6. Bake in pre-heated oven at 350°F/180°C for 12 minutes or until pale golden.

7. Cool on wire rack and store in an airtight container.

Makes about 30 biscuits.

Jane: We found some potted meat and biscuits and Worcester sauce, and the tongue doesn't look too bad.
Joe: (taking the tray from Jane) It isn't its looks I object to, it's its personality.

Cavalcade

Lady Stagg-Mortimer: …I should like a tongue sandwich, but no sherry. Sherry is the beginning of the end.

Post-Mortem

ACKNOWLEDGEMENTS

A special thank you to my sister-in-law and friend Dee Gorring who gave me a copy of *The Noël Coward Diaries* for my thirtieth birthday. It's been read so often it is falling apart. In Singapore I started the ANZA Writers Group and many of the original members are still in touch. All excellent writers, their support has been invaluable. That's you - Alison Stuart, Linda Collins, Johanna Leahy Marstrand, Rebecca Poston, Sue Flotow and Jane Riley.

My friend Lisa Rayner keeps me motivated with her generous praise. Diana Hockley and Niall Davidson have kindly read, critiqued and helped with editing. Robert Hazle, Cultural Development Officer for the Noël Coward Foundation, has been very supportive and encouraging. Andy McDermott from Publicious is a mine of information regarding publishing. Artist Rodney Greenstreet has drawn the illustrations – I'm very grateful for his contribution to the book. I thank all those from the 'Friends of Noël Coward' group and other friends, family and acquaintances who have shown an interest in this project and encouraged me to keep going.

BIBLIOGRAPHY & REFERENCES

Some of these provide quotations, others have inspired comments and recipes

Present Indicative – Noël Coward Heinemann1937

Future Indefinite – Noël Coward Heinemann1954

The Noël Coward Diaries – edited by Graham Payn and Sheridan Morley Weidenfeld & Nicloson 1982

Noël Coward: A Biography – Philip Hoare The University of Chicago Press 1995

Noël Coward and his friends – Cole Lesley, Graham Payn & Sheridan Morley Weidenfeld & Nicolson 1979

Remembered Laughter – Cole Lesley Alfred A. Knopf, Inc. New York 1976

My Life with Noël Coward – Graham Payn with Barry Day 1994 Applause Books 1996

Play Parade Volume Three The collected plays of Noël Coward Heinemann1950

Relative Values by Noël Coward Heinemann1952

Private Lives by Noël Coward

Delightful Food by Marjorie Salter & Adrianne Allen Whitney Sidgwick & Jackson, London 1957

The Fabulous Lunts – A Biography of Alfred Lunt and Lynn Fontanne by Jared Brown Athenium New York 1988

Mario of the Caprice An Autobiography by Mario Gallati Hutchinson of London 1960

Play Parade – Noël Coward Doubleday, Doran & Company, Inc.1934

Noël Coward Collected Verse Edited and introduced by Graham Payne and Martin Tickner Methuen 1999

The Wit of Noël Coward – Dick Richards Frewin 1968

Woman's Own Cook Book (1964) George Newnes Limited

The Pleasures of the Table – Sir Francis Colchester-Wemyss 1931

The All New Fannie Farmer Boston Cooking School Cookbook – COMPLETE AND UNABRIDGED – 1957

Classic British Dishes – Marguerite Patten1994 Bloomsbury Publishing Plc, 2 Soho Square, London WIV 6HB

Annie's Edwardian Cookery Book – Joan M. Haine 1972 Pelham Books Ltd 52 Bedford Square London W.C.1

French Provincial Cooking – Elizabeth David1960 Penguin Books Ltd, 27 Wrights Lane, London W8 5TZ England

French Country Cooking – Elizabeth David 1951 (as above)

Down to Earth Jamaican Cooking by Laurice de Gale 1996 Sister Vision, Black Women and Women of Colour Press; P.O. Box 217, Station E;Toronto, Ontario;

Canada M6H 4E2;(416) 595 5033

Our Favourite Dish – the theatre recipe book (1952) – Mrs Prince Littler Edited by Naomi Waters Putnam & Co Ltd

ABOUT THE AUTHOR

Julie Vellacott lives in the lovely Scenic Rim in south east Queensland. She has been a long-time admirer of Nöel Coward since listening to her oldest brother and friends sing his songs around the piano.

She is a keen reader, traveller, writer and wildlife watcher. Also, a hopeful photographer. Food, cooking and writing have been important in her life for both leisure and work. Julie has worked in several countries in the hospitality, entertainment, publishing and teaching fields.

Julie is passionate about theatre and all the arts. She collects vintage cookbooks and has dipped into them to unearth recipes for this book.

Julie retired recently from employment as a cultural officer and shares her home with Tiggomy – a very large, opinionated ginger cat.